Helping Teens
from
Alcoholic Families

Classroom Strategies for
Middle and High School Educators

By Jill Gover, Ph.D.

JOHNSON INSTITUTE®

Helping Teens from Alcoholic Families
Classroom Strategies for Middle and High School Educators

Johnson Institute – QVS, Inc.
7205 Ohms Lane
Minneapolis, MN 55439-2159
(612) 831-1630

ISBN: 1-56246-059-5

Printed in the United States of America.

Acknowledgments

This book would not have been possible without the help of my mentor and dear friend, Jewel Fink. She sparked the initial concept for this book and prodded me along when times got rough. Her unswerving belief in me and our vision of hope for children growing up in chemically dependent families has been a constant source of inspiration.

I wish to thank the Gover clan—especially Hank, Henrietta, Ann, and Skye—for their encouragement, support, and assistance with manuscript preparation.

My heartfelt thanks goes also to Jim Kirkpatrick, my first "teacher" who got me started doing this work and so generously fostered my professional growth.

In addition, a very big thank you goes to Jean Pettit and Doreen Monroe, who laboriously typed, edited, and retyped the entire manuscript. Gratitude is also extended to the staff at Johnson Institute, especially Jim Bitney and Carol Danielson, for their perceptive editing and valuable feedback, which helped get this manuscript into print.

Most importantly, I dedicate this book to the children and staff in the Vallejo Unified School District, who have nurtured and taught me so much. Through my work in the schools, they have given me much more than I can ever return. Most especially, I thank the COAs who participated in my groups for sharing their inner selves.

About the Author

For more than 20 years, F. Jill Gover, Ph.D., has worked with adolescents and their families as an educator, counselor, and clinical psychologist. Since 1982 she has been leading and supervising groups for school-age children and adolescents living in chemically dependent families. Dr. Gover has been instrumental in developing school programs for children of alcoholics and addicts (COAs), and she currently supervises alcohol and other drug intervention and treatment programs for the Vallejo Unified School District.

Contents

Introduction

There are approximately 28 million children of alcoholics (COAs) living in the United States (Robinson, 1989). The number of COAs under the age of 18 ranges from 7 million to 15 million (Towers, 1989)—the equivalent of four children in every classroom.

School-age children living in chemically dependent homes face a difficult struggle. Bryan Robinson, in his book *Working with Children of Alcoholics,* uses a battle metaphor to describe the lives of these children. They are like prisoners of war held hostage in a hostile country with little hope of escape. These children grow up struggling to survive the psychological war raging in their families. They gather their ammunition, erect their barricades, and stand vigilant, waiting for battle. Frequently they are ambushed by the chemical dependent's broken promises, mood swings, inconsistent behavior, and manipulation. Oftentimes they carry the emotional and physical scars of violence and abuse. These are children caught in the crossfire, and they suffer as soldiers do.

Some children become war heroes, the generals who plan strategies for survival and keep the troops together in the midst of chaos (family hero). Some end up foot soldiers in hand-to-hand combat with the enemy, fighting for their lives (scapegoat). Others survive by entertaining the troops (mascot). And still others become the "missing-in-action" (lost child). Regardless of rank, they all are casualties.

The sooner these children get help, the better their chance of surviving the war or even escaping to neutral territory. Critical to a child's healthy social and emotional development is the bonding with a significant, caring adult (Hawkins, 1989). Usually such bonding occurs with a parent, but if a parent is not available, any caring adult can make the difference between resiliency (surviving the war) and risk (becoming war damaged). This book presents specific ways that teachers and other school staff members can reach out and help these children on the battlefield. As educators, we can choose to ignore the carnage, but it will affect our classrooms, nevertheless. We are all affected, directly or indirectly, by alcohol and other drug use.

The purpose of this publication is to help teachers and other school staff members understand the deleterious effects of growing up in a chemically dependent home. This book aims to raise awareness of the needs and characteristics of COAs and to explain how educators can help. In the following pages, I will discuss:

- the disease concept of alcoholism
- the psychological effects of living in a chemically dependent family
- how to identify COAs
- how to avoid becoming a professional enabler
- what to do for help
- where to go for information and materials.

The content is a synthesis of my clinical work with children of chemical dependents and the latest research. It is an outgrowth of my desire to help educators touch the lives of children in need and ultimately improve services to COAs everywhere.

1 The Family as a System

A family consists of a group of people who are interrelated. The members of a family operate in an interdependent system. Like any other system, the family has a body of parts that work together. A healthy family has certain characteristics that make it function well as a system. Healthy families have developed a foundation of love and trust. They have clear communication between and among members that allows them to identify and express a range of feelings. Healthy, functional families don't insist on conformity and rigid behavior codes; rather, they promote compromise and negotiation in order to resolve conflicts. All family members share a sense of mutual respect and input and participation. However, it is clear to all involved that the parents are in control. Each member of the family has clearly defined limits ("This is how far I'll go") and boundaries ("This is how far I'll let you go"), and everyone pulls his or her own weight to contribute to the family system.

Imagine the healthy family as being like a mobile—flexible and changing and adapting to different external conditions. Pieces of the mobile change positions and shift with the wind, but they always remain connected to each other. For example, if the wind moves or sets one part of the mobile off balance, the whole system shifts gradually to bring itself back to equilibrium. In a family, this shifting and search for balance is called homeostasis. When life's "winds" create stress in one member of the family, the entire family shifts to bring stability back to the system. The strings of a well-functioning mobile are connected at the top but are not tangled. Each piece of the mobile is allowed a wide range of individual movement. The same is true of a well-functioning family. All the members are connected and are affected by each other's behavior, but there isn't a constricted, tangled, "enmeshed" feeling. The family mobile is free, flexible, and balanced.

However, when one or more family members are not functioning well because of addictive and compulsive behaviors, the whole family becomes dysfunctional. Although there are many different addictive and compulsive behaviors that create a dysfunctional family system (for example, mood disorders, eating disorders, compulsive gambling, sex and love addiction, certain mental illnesses, religious fanaticism, or physical abuse of one or more members of a family), dysfunctional families are most often associated with alcohol and other drug dependence. In dysfunctional families, the family mobile isn't allowed to flow and sway in the breeze. Instead, each family member adapts or shifts to the behavior of the chemically dependent person (or the person suffering from the disorder) by developing ways of coping that allow him or her to survive in the family system. Everyone's focus is on the chemically dependent person who, in turn, is exclusively focused on maintaining his or her chemical use. The family member who is dependent on alcohol or other drugs* is no longer pulling his or her own weight and contributing to the family. The rest of the family shifts to accommodate, but the balance is off. Boundaries and limits get confused. Free expression of feelings and open communication become dangerous and unacceptable. The strings of the family mobile get tangled, enmeshed, and rigid. Finally, the entire system breaks down.

Chemical Dependence— Disease in the Family

Not too long ago, alcoholism was viewed as a character flaw. People who drank too much were told that they were weak and morally inferior. In other words, there was something wrong with people who could not control their use of alcohol. Now we know that alcoholism is a disease. In fact, the American Medical Association,

---

*You'll notice that we use the term "alcohol and other drug(s)" throughout this book. We do so to emphasize that alcohol is a drug—just like cocaine, marijuana, amphetamines, depressants, or any other mind-altering chemical. Too often we hear people talk about alcohol or drugs or alcohol and drugs as if alcohol were somehow different from drugs and belonged to a category all by itself. True, our culture, our government, even our laws treat alcohol differently from the way they treat other drugs such as pot, crack, or heroin. But the symptoms of addiction are basically the same for all of these mind-altering chemicals, and the need to find ways to prevent their use is just as urgent. When we use the term "chemical dependence," it covers addiction to any of these mind-altering chemicals.

American Psychiatric Association, American Psychological Association, American Public Health Association, National Association of Social Workers, and the World Health Organization have all officially declared alcoholism to be a disease. Moreover, research is substantiating evidence that people who have a history of alcoholism in their family may have a genetic predisposition to the disease.

Whether a person is using alcohol or any other drug, the symptoms of chemical dependence are essentially the same. A chemically dependent person is one who is dependent on a mind-altering chemical to function normally and who continues to use despite negative consequences. This person is physiologically and psychologically addicted to a chemical ingested or absorbed into the body that impairs thoughts, feelings, and behavior. Chemical dependence is considered a disease that is primary, progressive, chronic, and, if not treated, fatal.

Chemical dependence is not a secondary symptom of another illness. It is a primary disease in that the addiction causes physical illness, disturbed family relationships, depression, trouble in the workplace, and other problems. The chemical use must first stop before these problems can be resolved. Moreover, chemical dependence is an obsessive-compulsive behavior that dominates the user's thinking ("Where can I get some?" "Where will I hide my supply?"). Chemical dependence gets worse over time. The chemically dependent person becomes emotionally, spiritually, and physically ill as the disease progresses. This disease can only be arrested, not eradicated. It is a chronic condition that can be treated by involvement in a lifelong process called recovery, which is based on abstinence from all mind-altering chemicals. If not treated, a person may eventually die from chemical dependence or related behaviors.

Continuum of Use

Experimental Use	Social Use	Relief Use	Abuse	Chemical Dependence

Although everyone starts with experimental use, different people move through the continuum of use at different rates. For a variety of reasons, some people may stop at social use, while others will progress rapidly along the continuum to chemical dependence. On the average, it takes an adult approximately seven years to reach full-blown alcoholism, whereas adolescents can complete the continuum in two years or less.

In the early phases of use, people have a choice whether or not to use alcohol or other drugs. Those who decide to use do so in order to experience a positive mood swing. "Just Say No" campaigns are often aimed at this population. However, as people move along the continuum from experimental use to social use to relief use, many cross an invisible line into addiction or chemical dependence. The chemical takes control, and people can no longer decide to use or not to use. They must have the chemical to cope with their feelings. Eventually, as they move from abuse into chemical dependence, their bodies demand the drug, and they must have it in order to function normally.

Stages of the Disease of Chemical Dependence

There are four stages in the progression of the disease of chemical dependence:

- Stage I: Learning the Mood Swing (Experimental Use)
- Stage II: Seeking the Mood Swing (Social Use)
- Stage III: Harmful Dependence (Relief Use—Abuse)
- Stage IV: Chemical Dependence

Stage I begins the continuum of use (Experimental Use). The user learns that the chemical provides euphoric mood swings. In Stage II: Seeking the Mood Swing (Social Use), the user seeks the euphoric feelings but develops self-imposed rules and adheres to them. For example, the social user will say, "I won't drink on week nights" and drink only on the weekends. She or he may experience negative physical consequences (for example, a hangover) but no emotional pain as a result of drinking. Although the social user can control the time and quantity of alcohol or other drug use, his or her tolerance for the chemical increases with continued use.

Stage III marks the transition into harmful dependence. The person in Stage III uses the chemical to numb emotional pain (Relief Use). However, as she or he experiences periodic loss of control over use (Abuse), behavior associated with that use violates the person's value system and causes *more* emotional pain. For example, a man who believes it is wrong to hit a woman but who punches his girlfriend when drunk will feel guilty afterwards. However, he will deny that his drinking had anything to do with his behavior. Instead he'll think to himself, "I hit her because she got me mad, not because I was drunk." To assuage his guilt, the man will drink more, hoping to relieve the emotional pain and stress his behavior is causing him. If he continues to drink despite negative consequences, his lifestyle will change and begin to revolve around his drinking. Self-imposed rules like "I won't drink on week nights" will be broken. He'll drink when he's upset, and he'll be upset more and more frequently as the cycle spins out of control. As the person's tolerance for the drug increases, he or she may engage in illegal or deceitful behavior in order to acquire greater quantities of the drug. The user's self-esteem drops. She or he denies a problem with chemicals and begins to project self-hatred onto others, blaming everyone and everything else for her or his troubles.

By the time Stage IV: Chemical Dependence occurs, the person is using chemicals simply to feel normal. What started out as a search for the euphoric "high" is now an attempt to function normally. Blackouts often occur in this stage. The person doesn't remember what transpires during these blackout periods. The person is physiologically addicted; the body craves the drug. Paranoid thinking develops, especially with certain chemicals such as cocaine and amphetamines. At this point, the chemically dependent (CD) is often suicidal, having lost the desire to live. Continued use at this end of the continuum will eventually result in death.

Stages of the Disease in the Family

Besides the individual user, chemical dependence also adversely affects all members of the family. As the disease progresses, the family system becomes more and more dysfunctional. The disintegration of a functional family follows a predictable pattern and can be categorized into four stages:

- Stage I: Denial
- Stage II: Attempts to Control
- Stage III: Disorganization
- Stage IVa: Disassociation

    or

    Stage IVb: Divorce

    or

    Stage IVc: Recovery and Reorganization

Stage I: Denial. In this stage, all family members are involved in a "conspiracy of silence." The family priority at this point is to hide the problem. The CD exhibits periodic instances of inappropriate intoxicated behavior, but it is not a chronic state. At this point, family members feel embarrassed and angry at the CD when these incidents occur. There are often long discussions, pleas, and broken promises. The alcohol or other drug problem is usually hidden from the younger children. The spouse will tend to seek advice from friends or family on how to control the partner's chemical use.

Stage II: Attempts to Control. In this stage, the family works to keep the problem "in the family." The family focuses on isolating and controlling the problem use. The family feels helpless but is determined to solve the problem *alone*. The CD continues to use, and inappropriate behavior becomes more severe and more frequent. The spouse attempts to control use by controlling the money or using chemicals with the CD. Family members may hide, throw out, or destroy the chemical- and drug-related paraphernalia. Children begin to show signs of being adversely affected. School performance may drop, frequent arguments and fights occur, and moody, tense attitudes develop.

14

Family members think they are the cause of the problem. Often kids think, "It's my fault that Dad's drinking so much and Mom and he are fighting all the time." It's common during this stage for the first medical or legal crisis to occur. The CD may get his or her first D.U.I. (Driving Under the Influence) citation, break a leg from falling drunk, get injured in a fight while high, and so on. As more negative consequences occur, the CD's relationship with family members continues to deteriorate.

Stage III: Disorganization. By the time the family has progressed into Stage III, family life is chaotic. All of the family's energy is focused on keeping the family together. Family members feel too scared to act and too scared not to act, emotionally paralyzed by the situation. At this point, the CD has progressed to the middle-late stage of the disease (Stages III-IV of the disease continuum). He or she exhibits behaviors associated with harmful dependence. In response, the family takes over the chemically dependent person's responsibilities. Although the family system adjusts to the "weight" of the CD, everyone feels afraid, resentful, and indecisive. Medical or legal crises continue, and violence may occur more and more frequently. Family members adopt survival roles (see Chapter 2) to deal with the increased chaos and isolation.

If the family doesn't get help by Stage III, it will progress either to Stage IVa: Disassociation or to Stage IVb: Divorce. With appropriate help, however, the family will shift to Stage IVc: Recovery and Reorganization.

Stage IVa: Disassociation. Movement to this stage occurs when the family accepts the chemical dependence as a permanent condition and copes by avoiding the CD as much as possible. The CD, at this point, has progressed to the late stages of the continuum of use and is using now to feel normal rather than to get high. The family has resigned itself to this situation and ignores the chemically dependent person as much as possible. The spouse controls the finances, but usually there are financial problems because the CD is not financially responsible. Survival roles (see Chapter 2) become ingrained behavior patterns. Family members live in constant chronic fear of crisis and/or violence. Guilt and resentment grow.

Stage IVb: Divorce. If the sober parent cannot or will not disassociate from the chemically dependent partner, he or she will divorce or separate in order to get away from the chemical abuse and to reorganize the family. The CD will escalate attempts to charm, seduce, or frighten the family back. Unfortunately, the spouse is usually still hooked into the CD emotionally, worrying about his or her safety, physical condition, mental state, and the like. The survival roles will continue even though the CD is gone because feelings of guilt, fear, and resentment remain.

There is hope, however. If there is an intervention, and the family seeks counseling, there is always a chance to reintegrate the family. An intervention is a caring process that usually culminates in a powerful confrontation with the CD, seeking to convince him or her to get professional help. An intervention may involve one or several people, depending on the objective (what those involved hope to achieve) and the type of intervention. There are three types of intervention: (1) professional; (2) mutual aid group; and (3) concerned persons. Professional interventions are formal and organized by a mental health professional. A mutual aid group intervention is led by people in recovery from chemical dependence who invite the CD to attend meetings with them. A concerned persons' intervention is conducted by a group of people who care and are willing to confront and convince the CD to get help. There are advantages and considerations for each type of intervention, but all interventions share the common goal of convincing the CD to get outside help in order to stop using, the first step toward recovery from chemical dependence.

Stage IVc: Recovery and Reorganization. For a family to reach this stage, the chemically dependent member must first abstain from chemicals. Even when the chemical use ceases, however, destructive behaviors will persist for a long time. That is the difference between being "dry" (not using) and recovering (involvement in a process of healing). Initially there will be a honeymoon period when everyone is happy that the CD has stopped using. However, the family may resist the CD's attempts to regain responsibilities and shift roles. Family members have gotten used to carrying more than their weight and may not be willing to give up the control, fearing that the CD will disappoint them once again and act irresponsibly. It takes a long time for family members to begin to forgive the CD and develop the trust that chemical use has destroyed.

Chemical dependence is a term used to describe the condition of being "hooked on drugs." Don't forget that alcohol is a drug too. When a person becomes dependent on alcohol or other drugs, his or her entire life revolves around obtaining and using that drug. The person's primary relationship is with that drug, not with anyone or anything else. How do you know if a person has crossed that invisible line into chemical dependence? If the use of alcohol or any other drug is causing disruption or problems in a person's physical, emotional, financial, or spiritual life, and the person continues to use despite the negative consequences, it is safe to conclude that the person can no longer decide not to use. The loss of choice is the result of dependence.

Unfortunately, not just the person using the drug is hurt by chemical dependence. Because the person is part of a family system, *everyone* in that system is adversely affected. Children growing up in this environment suffer silently, coping the best they can with an unpredictable, stressful, and frightening reality. In order to survive, they develop an armor of protection, a wall of defenses, and an army of survival roles to protect themselves from their painful feelings. Chapter 2 will discuss these survival roles in detail.

2 Survival Roles

As we've seen, the family is part of a complex environmental system. If a family member is chemically dependent, his or her primary relationship is with his or her chemical of choice, and the person doesn't carry his or her own weight or function effectively in the family. To compensate, other family members assume roles that unintentionally allow the CD to continue his or her chemically dependent behavior. To survive the chaos, family members adopt roles and rigidly adhere to them as the family becomes more and more dysfunctional. These roles create a wall of defenses designed to protect each family member.

The Chemically Dependent

The CD uses alcohol and other drugs as an easy escape and relief from the pains and burdens of life, rather then developing and using skills to cope with difficulties in a constructive manner. Operating under an unspoken motto, "Don't look at me!" the chemically dependent family member attempts to deflect attention away from his or her real problem (chemical use) by creating chronic chaos within the family. The CD's outer wall of defenses compulsively covers up real feelings. This coverup results in a cycle of self-delusion and denial. Consequently, others in the family pick up the double message, sensing the real feelings that are denied and repressed, but hearing the projected set of defenses. This causes confusion and self-doubt. Because these repressed feelings are not consciously available to anyone, a growing action/reaction develops between the family and the CD, exacerbating the self-delusional process. The family becomes more and more out of touch with reality.

CDs project a wall of defenses, including blaming others (external locus of control), grandiosity (unrealistic goals), perfectionist expectations of self and others, rigid black-or-white thinking, demanding self-righteous beliefs, and manipulative, charming, and seductive behaviors (especially when obtaining the chemical of choice). The CD's grandiose schemes coupled with a rigid, perfectionist attitude are often a setup for failure, which the CD then uses as an excuse to drink or get high in order to numb the painful feelings associated with the failure.

Inside, CDs feel alone, hurt, scared, worthless, and guilty about what they have done as a consequence of their chemical use. What they need is unconditional love coupled with supportive confrontation. They need to be given responsibility and validated for their strengths. At the same time, however, they also need to be held accountable for their actions. As long as they are rescued by others, they will not experience the consequences of their use.

The Chief Enabler

Enabling means "to give power to; to allow." In the context of chemical dependence, enabling involves those ideas, feelings, attitudes, and behaviors that unwittingly allow alcohol and other drug problems to continue by preventing the user from experiencing the consequences of his or her use in order to sustain one's own well-being. Without the appropriate information and awareness, family members, friends, co-workers, and the community can all enable the CD to continue using. (Note: Chapter 6 will discuss enabling in greater depth.)

In a chemically dependent family, generally there is one person who plays the role of chief enabler. For example, if Dad is alcoholic, Mom frequently assumes the role of chief enabler— single-handedly running the family, protecting and covering up for Dad, and essentially doing the jobs of two people in the family. As a result, Mom experiences burnout and feels inadequate, confused, fearful, resentful, and angry. The chief enabler is usually the spouse, but not always. In a single-parent family, for example, the chief enabler is usually the oldest child.

The chief enabler can also be called the *primary co-dependent* because the CD relies on this person most heavily. A co-dependent is any person who has an ongoing relationship with a chemically dependent person that causes debilitating stress and compulsive behavior. A co-dependent may not be living with the CD, but as long as this person is willing to be of "help" when sought out by the CD during a continuing series of crises, he or she may be considered co-dependent. People who are not co-dependent will detach and refuse to remain involved once they recognize that the CD is not willing to follow through, change behavior, or take responsibility for himself or herself. Co-dependents, on the other hand, will maintain an unhealthy relationship, shield the CD from the harmful consequences of his or her using, and deny or minimize the seriousness of the situation.

As the disease progresses, chief enablers become more enmeshed with the CD. Their lives revolve around the CD, and they become obsessed with their efforts to change, control, manipulate, or compensate for the CD's destructive behavior. Their function in the family is to maintain control at any cost, and their unspoken motto is "Poor Me!" On the outside, they are controlling, manipulative, super-responsible, fragile, and suffering—the "martyr."

Chief enablers do what they do because there is a payoff. In their misguided attempts to keep the family together, chief enablers often feel self-righteous, responsible, and important. However, chief enablers feel angry at and abandoned by the CD, guilty for *not* keeping it all together, hurt, afraid, exhausted, overwhelmed, and victimized by the situation. What chief enablers need is to learn how to take care of themselves, to detach from the CD, to focus on their own needs, and to identify their own feelings. Essentially, they need to learn how to stop enabling.

The Family Hero*

The oldest child often takes on the survival role of family hero, a super-popular and successful overachiever who tries to be perfect so that a parent will stop using alcohol and other drugs. The family hero can never succeed, so he or she ends up feeling inadequate, confused, frustrated, and hurt. Family heroes are also called the "looking-good kids," because they make the family look good on

---

*The following roles are originally from Sharon Wegscheider-Cruse, *The Family Trap*, Minneapolis: Nurturing Networks, 1979.

the outside. They are also called "caretakers" because they attempt to fix the family's pain by taking care of everybody. They become hypervigilant about everything that is happening and seek approval and self-worth through external successes defined by others.

The difference between the family hero and a successful person is that family heroes feel worthless, inadequate, and defeated inside, because their valiant efforts fail to stop the disintegration of the family as the disease of chemical dependence progresses. Others would describe these children as approval-seeking, independent, successful, high-achieving, special, all-together, perfectionist, and super-responsible. Family heroes' outer wall of defenses masks the confusion, hurt, and inadequacy underneath. Because their self-esteem is so tied to external success, family heroes can be at risk for suicide if they experience any kind of perceived failure, such as failing a test or not being accepted into a college of choice.

The Scapegoat

A second survival role of children in chemically dependent families is the scapegoat, the "bad" kid. This person absorbs the blame for the family's dysfunction. He or she refuses to compete with the family hero and reacts oppositionally, looking for support outside the family, among peers. The scapegoat's function in the family is to keep the focus off the CD by providing a focus for the family on which members can dump their anger. With the motto "I'll show you!" the scapegoat gets into trouble, acts out the family's pain and anger, and unintentionally distracts the family from the real problem. The wall of defenses the scapegoat shows includes acting out, defiance, and self-destructive behaviors (for example, bullying others, unplanned pregnancy, alcohol or other drug abuse, and so on). Like the CD, the scapegoat is angry, sullen, and aloof, blaming others for all problems. Frequently, the scapegoat suffers failure in school, behavior problems, and a strong, negative peer group association.

Inside, the scapegoat feels rejected, hurt, worthless, afraid, lonely, and confused. The scapegoat child needs structure, consistency, supportive confrontation, positive attention, opportunities for success, and limited choices that help him or her increase a sense of empowerment and autonomy.

The Lost Child

A third survival role, often adopted by the middle child in a CD family, is that of the lost child, the invisible, quiet one, whose purpose in the family is "not to be a burden." This is the child the family doesn't have to think about. By being very good and very quiet, these children fade into the background, masking their pain and loneliness behind a wall of disengagement. They retreat and withdraw when conflict arises. Because they never "rock the boat," lost children receive little attention or direction. As a result, they have a difficult time connecting with other people and sharing emotions, so their relationships tend to be shallow and unfulfilling. Lost children's internalized shame, alienation, and loneliness make them high risk for eating disorders, obesity, depression, and suicide. Outwardly, they appear removed, withdrawn, compliant, aloof, super-independent, and distant. Inwardly, they feel inadequate, hurt, angry, and painfully lonely.

Although lost children want more than anything to connect with others, they are extremely untrusting, preferring to reject than to be rejected. To form friendships, they need repeated invitations to risk the possibility of rejection. Moreover, they need encouragement, positive attention, lots of reassurance to participate in group activities, chances to take "safe" risks, and opportunities to feel accepted and be successful.

The Mascot

Frequently, the youngest child in a CD family takes on the fourth survival role, that of the mascot—the cute, mischievous, endearing class clown. The mascot's job in the family is to keep the focus off the chemical dependent's use and provide humor, fun, and diversion. The mascot's motto is "Look at me!" No one takes mascots too seriously, and they are often shielded or protected from what is really going on in the family. They provide amusement, affection, and distraction from the pervasive family pain. The mascot's wall of defenses projects a person who is humorous, fragile, charming, super-cute, hyperactive, and likely to do anything to attract attention. Those defenses cover up the mascot's true feelings of fear, insecurity, confusion, and helplessness. Mascots often struggle with emotional immaturity and dependence. They need to be taken seriously, included and consulted in family decision-making, and affirmed for their contributions.

* * * * * * *

Different family members take on different survival roles at different times in their lives. Many times, one person will adopt several roles at once. Sometimes a person will flip-flop between two roles. For example, a child may initially adopt the role of family hero, but as the family becomes more dysfunctional and frustration builds, the child may give up trying to be good and assume the role of scapegoat.

These survival roles reflect personality types that are familiar to all families. However, these roles become problematic when family members *get stuck* in them and are unable to act differently. In chemically dependent families, each family member gets locked into survival patterns and roles. These roles work well to protect the individuals from the painful feelings that are stuffed behind the wall of defenses. Because these roles develop into compulsive behaviors that are unconscious, family members act out the roles in all their relationships, not just in the family. The wall of defenses that mask the repressed feelings becomes a primary problem for each family member.

Survival roles emerge in dysfunctional families because members don't feel safe enough to communicate honestly. Each person reacts to another person in the system, and when one member is chemically dependent, everyone else adjusts, accommodates, and survives by adopting a role. However, the nature of the disease is such that denial prevents acknowledging what is really happening. Family members deceive themselves, believing what is not true, unaware of the survival roles they are in. These roles become compulsive self-destructive patterns in which specific behaviors characterize each family member. Although these roles are ways of coping with the pain and chaos of the home environment, each family member pays a high price to survive.

The chemically dependent becomes a slave to the chemical. The chief enabler becomes a martyr, sacrificing his or her own needs for the sake of others. The family hero feels driven and inadequate despite personal successes. The scapegoat engages in self-destructive behaviors. The lost child, alienated and alone, doesn't bond or connect with others. The mascot never learns responsibility. Everyone suffers from low self-esteem and unhappiness.

3 Psychological Effects of Living in a Chemically Dependent Family

Living in a chemically dependent family is very stressful. Chronic stress for prolonged periods of time causes profound psychological disturbances. No matter what survival role a child of an alcoholic or addict (COA) assumes, self-worth is nonexistent. COAs believe that their worth comes from events, things, or other people; their self-esteem is determined completely by *external* factors. When self-esteem is a function of behavior and the reaction of others, it's difficult to maintain an equilibrium. Self-worth or self-esteem needs to come from inside, through the innate belief that "I am a good person." Robert Reasoner (1982) identifies five essential elements of self-esteem:

1. A Sense of Security
2. A Sense of Identity
3. A Sense of Belonging
4. A Sense of Purpose
5. A Sense of Personal Competence

Living in a chemically dependent family negatively affects the development of all five of these senses.

A Sense of Security

COAs don't experience a sense of security in the home, because they never know what will happen when they walk in the door. One day chemically dependent Mom may greet little Jimmy with cookies and milk, and the next day she might be passed out on the floor. Chemically dependent people are not capable of effective parenting. They cannot set or consistently enforce family rules. Their discipline is arbitrary, capricious, and unpredictable. Living in such a home is like walking on eggshells. There is no stability, predictable routine, or clear expectations. At any moment, Mom or Dad could start drinking or using, and then everything changes. Promises are frequently broken. Children interpret such parental behavior as judgments on their worth as human beings. Children feel shame, believing that their parents regard them as "bad kids." Shame-filled children no longer feel secure in their families, and their self-esteem suffers mightily.

A Sense of Identity

Children initially develop their sense of identity from the feedback of significant others. When parents are intoxicated or high, they often say things they don't really mean. Their thought processes are impaired, judgment blurred, and inhibitions lowered. As a result, chemically dependent parents can say very cruel and hurtful things in anger. Statements like "You're such a stupid kid!" or "You're so bad you drive me to drink!" are ways that a CD projects blame onto others. However, when children hear such statements from a parent, they internalize them and begin to define themselves in negative ways. This creates a poor self-image, which, in turn, lowers self-esteem. Moreover, a child identifies self in relation to family. Frequently children blame themselves for their parents' drinking or drug use. Feelings of inadequacy develop a negative self-concept, further increasing shame and lowering self-esteem.

A Sense of Belonging

A sense of belonging is critical for emotional health in all human beings. We all need to feel that we belong and are connected with other people. In a dysfunctional family, members don't find the belonging they need. Instead, they often feel alienated and alone. Although everyone in the family knows there is "an elephant in the living room" (that is, a family member who has an alcohol or other drug problem), no one divulges the family secret. This exacerbates feelings of being different, alone, and of not fitting in or belonging. Because children are told not to talk about the family secret, there is no way for them to share their feelings with others. This, too, prevents them from developing a sense of belonging.

A Sense of Purpose and Personal Competence

Dysfunctional family members rarely cultivate a sense of purpose and a sense of personal competence, because everyone is so consumed with controlling the drinking or other drug use that there is little energy left for anything else. The school environment might build academic competencies and career goals for the family hero. The lost child might experience personal competence by developing self-reliance as a coping strategy. However, the scapegoat and the mascot have little opportunity to build these areas of self-esteem.

In school the mascot, playing the role of class clown, rarely reflects on goals or skill acquisition. Because the mascot is always joking around, he or she rarely thinks seriously about the future. For the mascot, life is superficial, frivolous, and exists only in the moment. However, underneath the clown exterior, mascots are very fearful of the future, because they lack direction and purpose. Rather than respond thoughtfully to the question "What do I want to achieve in life?" the mascot suppresses the anxiety evoked by the question by joking or evading the subject.

The scapegoat, too, has little sense of purpose and perceives self as incompetent and worthless. The family blames the scapegoat for all the problems, which is why the term "scapegoat" is used to describe this role in the family (Cruse 1979). The child internalizes all the negativity and blame projected onto him or her. The scapegoat comes to believe Dad's or Mom's angry prediction "You will never amount to anything." Consequently, the scapegoat lacks hope for the future and is unable to articulate realistic goals or to aspire towards a dream. The scapegoat's absence of a sense of purpose lowers motivation and erodes self-esteem.

Family Rules

At a very early age, COAs learn three unspoken rules that they follow in order to survive in the family: (1) don't talk; (2) don't feel; and (3) don't trust (Black 1981). Children learn that it is not okay to talk about what is really happening in the family. This "conspiracy of silence" prevents the child from talking about the taboo subject. If the child breaks the family rule and does talk about the real problem (Dad's or Mom's alcohol or other drug use), the rest of the family denies the existence of any such problem and acts as if the child were crazy. This is very confusing for COAs, who then begin to doubt their own reality. Like a character in the story *The Emperor's New Clothes,* the COA thinks, "If everyone else perceives reality in a certain way that is different from what I see, *I must be crazy.*" To hide this terribly painful and confusing feeling, the COA learns not to talk about what is really happening.

Moreover, COAs learn to repress vulnerable feelings such as hurt, rejection, or sadness and to replace them with feelings associated with being powerful—rage, anger, and the like. In a chemically dependent family, aggressive feelings are the easiest to access, and thus, are the ones most often expressed. Other feelings (loneliness, fear, hurt, shame, pain, and the like) are "frozen" or "stuffed" out of consciousness, so COAs never learn to identify or express those feelings. Since confidence in oneself develops through self-acceptance and the appropriate expression of feelings, the COA's self-esteem is lowered even more.

Perhaps the most damaging rule in a dysfunctional family, however, is the third: don't trust. When a child's primary caregiver (parent) is chemically dependent, the child experiences repeated disappointment, broken promises, and inconsistent parenting. The child learns from these experiences not to trust people. If children can't trust their parents, they figure they can't trust anybody. Trust is fundamental to establishing relationships with others and self, so the inability to trust people creates a myriad of problems that carry over into adulthood.

Shame Versus Guilt

A COA's low self-esteem is exacerbated by a profound sense of shame, which is very different from guilt feelings. People feel guilty about events or behaviors they know are wrong and regret having done. Shame, however, causes people to feel bad about *who they are,* about the self. There are three dimensions of shame: (1) it is a primary feeling; (2) it is induced initially; and (3) it eventually becomes internalized.

Shame is a deeper, more primary emotion than guilt; it is not used to cover up other emotions or to keep people away. Anger, for example, is often used to mask vulnerable feelings like shame or hurt or fear that lie underneath. Initially, shame is induced by the reactions of others, particularly primary caregivers such as parents or other adults who are viewed as powerful. Eventually the shame becomes internalized, and the individual develops a belief system that is rooted in shame. Encompassed in shame are feelings of being exposed, "caught," embarrassed, trapped, and humiliated. Shame involves a loss of dignity and an extreme acute disappointment that is never discussed or appeased.

Of course, functional families also experience disappointment that damages relationships. However, in functional families, the damaged bonds are mended. Disappointments are followed by experiences that rebuild trust and repair the relationship. In dysfunctional families, however, the bonds are severed. Disappointment is followed only by more disappointment. Children who live in dysfunctional families, particularly those children trapped in the scapegoat role, often hide their shame by projecting blame; since they are unable to express verbally how wretched they feel about themselves (family rules #1: don't talk, and #2: don't feel), scapegoats will act out negative feelings by "dumping" them on others. Teachers, and other school personnel and caregivers who attempt to control the acting-out child by "pulling the choke collar," cornering the child, and "bullying" him or her into compliance, are unwittingly reinforcing that child's internal experience of shame. Chapter 4 will deal with this in greater detail.

The lives of COAs are seriously jeopardized by their family's problem. The crazier and more violent the home, the tougher it is to reach family members because their wall of defenses is more rigid and impermeable. The further family members have progressed in the stages of family disintegration, the greater they deny and minimize how bad things really are. They distort reality to cope with their pain. The resultant isolation makes COAs so needy that they are vulnerable to being victimized. No matter the type or quantity of the drug used, what role a family member assumes, or where family members are in the stages of family disintegration, *all* COAs suffer because they do not learn how to express feelings, affection, or intimacy with others. The "don't feel" rule prevents them from identifying and expressing true feelings.

Moreover, in a dysfunctional family, love is conditional, based on what one does. COAs don't learn how to give affection with no strings attached, because the affection they receive from the chemically dependent parent *has* strings attached. The COA learns from the parent to give affection only when required to do so or only to manipulate others to get something. As mentioned earlier, because the sober parent is focused on the CD—who is focused exclusively on the chemical—neither parent is able to give the children what they need emotionally. As a result, the children suffer from self-doubt, low self-esteem, and an inability to trust others. This prevents them from developing healthy, intimate relationships. Lacking these relationships, their lives are adversely affected in all its aspects.

4 Concerns of Adolescent COAs

Once adolescent COAs receive permission to talk, they express many fears and concerns related to living with a chemically dependent person. The seven top concerns most frequently cited by adolescent COAs, in order of priority, are

1. Worries about hereditary transmission of chemical dependence
2. How to get parents sober
3. How to survive conflict in the home
4. How their family's problem affects dating, friendships, and school reputation
5. How to live with the CD
6. How to develop survival skills without getting stuck in roles
7. Other issues such as physical or sexual abuse, domestic violence, depression, or suicide (Ackerman 1987)

Hereditary Transmission

The number one concern for adolescents is whether or not they will end up like their chemically dependent parent. Adolescents commonly say, "It will never happen to me!" (Black 1981). However, COAs need to know the facts. They *are,* in fact, at greater risk of developing alcohol and other drug dependence, eating disorders, attention deficits, stress-related illnesses, and suicidal behavior than are other children (Lehr and Schrock 1987). Research indicates that boys who have alcoholic fathers are four times more likely to become alcoholic than boys with nonalcoholic fathers, and girls who have alcoholic fathers are three times more likely to develop the disease than girls with nonalcoholic fathers (Seixas 1985). Although there is still controversy in the field, most professionals agree that there is a genetic vulnerability to alcoholism that may be a hereditary transmission of the disease. Recent research has even linked a specific gene to alcoholism.

When explaining genetic vulnerability to an adolescent, it is helpful to use the metaphor of the "tiger in the stomach." The metaphor derives from the following story:

> Some people are born with a tiger sleeping in their stomach. If they never drink alcohol or use other drugs, they will never wake up the sleeping tiger. However, every time they use, they run the risk of waking the tiger. If they use enough, eventually they will wake the tiger, who has been growing all the time that it's been sleeping. When the tiger is awake, it's a ferocious addiction that's difficult to tame or control. The only way to control the tiger is to put it to sleep. A person with a "tiger in the stomach" can never get rid of it. But a person can keep the tiger sleeping by not drinking alcohol or using other drugs.

Children of alcoholics or addicts are more likely to be born with sleeping tigers in their stomachs than are other children. Without help, fifty percent of these children will become chemical abusers later on in life (Crowley 1984).

Adolescent COAs need to know that because of their family history, they are at much greater risk than their friends to develop chemical dependence if they experiment with alcohol and other drugs. For all teens, the earlier the onset of first drug use, the greater the risk for later abuse. However, for COAs born with a "sleeping tiger," any drug use is a game of Russian roulette. If they wake up the tiger, they will become chemically dependent. The good news is that adolescent COAs can do something about this genetic predisposition to the disease. Just as a young woman who has a family history of osteoporosis can exercise and take calcium to reduce her risk of contracting osteoporosis later in life, so can a COA make healthy choices to reduce the risk of developing chemical dependence.

Getting Parents Sober— "Fixing" the Problem

Most adolescent COAs want to know what to do to get their parent(s) sober. One of the psychosocial tasks of adolescence is to develop autonomy and self-control. The parents in a dysfunctional family are unable to model this behavior, because the chemically dependent parent is struggling with issues of impulse control, and the sober parent is struggling to control the CD. The child who is eager to please may never experience success because of the inconsistency of his or her parents' expectations.

Adolescence is also the time for developing a sense of responsibility for others. Teens in a dysfunctional family often take on an overwhelming, inappropriate level of responsibility in an attempt to maintain control and exert autonomy. Inevitably, however, these young people (family heroes) fail to control the CD's use. This failure increases their sense of helplessness. Nevertheless, their desire to "fix" the chemically dependent parent can keep them emotionally overinvolved with a dysfunctional family system well into adulthood.

Separation from the family is especially difficult for the adolescent who is filled with the self-doubt, inadequacy, low self-esteem, and anxiety that accompany the unreasonable level of responsibility expected in a chemically dependent home. It's difficult for teenagers to develop a normal sense of mastery when they feel responsible for events that are outside their control. Therefore, to address the concern "How do I get my parent(s) sober?" adolescents need to understand the "Three Cs":

1. You didn't Cause your parent's drinking or drug use.

2. You can't Control your parent's drinking or drug use.

3. You can't Cure or "fix" your parent.

Actually, there is a fourth C that can help teenage COAs: You Can learn to live your own life chemical-free, whether or not your parent ever gets sober.

COAs need to recognize that they cannot control other people's behavior, and that no matter what they do, they will never be able to get their parent(s) sober. Only the CD can make the decision to get well. When teens understand that enabling is *not* helping, and that the best way to "get a parent sober" is to *stop* enabling and *start* taking care of self, they will make healthier choices.

Surviving Conflict in the Home

Conflict tends to be frequent and severe in dysfunctional families. Chaos and unpredictability, poor communication, and chronic stress characterize the family atmosphere. Parental fighting, family arguments, and conflicts that escalate into physical violence are common occurrences. Teens want to know how to deal with potentially dangerous situations. They need to devise a plan of action that will help them take care of themselves. Such a plan could consist of calling or visiting certain designated friends or neighbors if the going gets rough at home, connecting with relatives who live nearby, or discussing their concerns with the sober parent. Being prepared helps reduce feelings of helplessness, fear, and anxiety. Anticipating potential conflict and brainstorming ways to avoid or defuse the conflict builds an internal locus of control—"I am not a victim of my circumstances; I can take care of myself."

Effects on Relationships and Reputation

By nature adolescents are egocentric. As such, they are often more concerned with how their chemically dependent parent's disease will affect *their life* than what will happen to the CD. They don't care so much about Dad's drinking or Mom's drug use, per se. What they do care about are the negative behaviors that result from the use—the fighting, financial problems, or embarrassing behavior that might reflect on them. Peer relationships are most important during adolescence. If Mom or Dad's behavior causes embarrassment, the adolescent is not likely to bring friends or dates home. No adolescent would ever risk being embarrassed in front of peers. That's why it's so important to break "the conspiracy of silence" and get kids *talking* to each other, so that they can form a social support network and get over the embarrassment they feel about their parent's behavior. The embarrassment diminishes when peers are understanding.

COAs who are talking about their parents' alcohol or other drug problem can truly empathize with each other: "I know how that feels. I thought I'd die when my dad...." Listening to each other, teenage COAs realize they are *not* responsible for their parents' behavior, and therefore have no reason to feel ashamed over it.

Living with a Chemically Dependent Parent and Developing Survival Skills

Adolescents want to know how to live with a chemically dependent parent. It isn't easy! Young people need to learn that the first step is to get help for themselves. Understanding the disease of chemical dependence and its effects on the family is a good beginning. This needs to be followed up by learning survival skills. Communication techniques, self-esteem enhancers, and team-building activities that increase trust are important survival skills for adolescent COAs. They need experiences outside the home (in school and in the community) to counteract the toxic interactions at home.

Because COAs repeatedly hear negative messages from the chemically dependent parent, they tend to suffer from several cognitive distortions. They often exhibit faulty logic such as black-and-white, all-or-none thinking, refusing to entertain the possibility of a "gray area." Moreover, they tend to overgeneralize. For example, many COAs tend to conclude that all people are untrustworthy, because one person betrayed their trust one time. COAs are also good at "catastrophizing," deducing Armageddon from one negative experience (Beck 1976). Although many "normal" teenagers exaggerate and distort thinking, teenage COAs are especially prone to creating faulty belief systems. Teaching critical thinking strategies helps correct faulty logic and, therefore, is another way to develop survival skills in COAs.

Other Issues of Concern

Adolescents who are dealing with specific issues related to physical or sexual abuse, domestic violence, and depression or suicide may need special therapy to heal from the traumas they've experienced. Alcohol and other drug problems are often associated with other dysfunctions in a family. For example, depression is very highly correlated with chemical abuse, and, in many cases, the CD is self-medicating with drugs to ease the pain caused by an affective mood disorder. If CDs have a dual diagnosis of chemical abuse and depression, their children are biologically vulnerable to depression. Biological depression needs to be treated by a professional, often with antidepressants.

* * * * * * *

Adolescent COAs have some very serious and very real concerns about chemical dependence and its impact on their lives. They need someone safe to talk to about these problems, and many times that special someone is a teacher. However, knowing how to respond appropriately is essential. Moreover, adolescent COAs require teaching strategies and classroom management techniques that aren't necessarily included in traditional teacher training. Many educators don't know how to engage this difficult population in the learning process effectively. Chapter 5 outlines ways for teachers to deal with these issues and to help adolescent COAs.

5 Working with Adolescent COAs: What to Do in the Classroom

In recent years, teachers have felt the pressure of various educational reforms that emphasize intellectual development. Unfortunately, such reforms fail to address the needs of the whole child. These needs include personal, social, and emotional development as well as intellectual development. Education that focuses only on academic mastery and standardized test scores does not take into account how difficult it is for a student to concentrate on algebra equations when he or she is worrying about whether or not Mom will get drunk, fall asleep with a lit cigarette, and burn down the house. Students cannot achieve their academic potential if personal or emotional problems interfere with learning.

One out of every five school-aged students is the child of a parent abusing alcohol or other drugs (Cox and Morehouse). That means that in a classroom of thirty students, six are COAs. Research has shown that these students are overrepresented among underachievers, truants, and behavior problems. Without help, COAs develop low self-esteem (DiCiccio, Davis, and Orenstein 1984), external locus of control (Kern, Hassett, and Collipp 1981), anxiety disorders (Cork 1969), depression (Moos and Billings 1982), chemical dependence (Morehouse and Scola 1986), compulsive need to control (Robinson 1989), and the inability to trust or maintain intimate relationships (Black 1981). Compared to children from nonalcoholic homes, COAs have more frequent changes in schools (Schulsinger, Knop, Goodwin, Teasdale, and Mikkelsen 1986), poor concentration (Tarter et al. 1984), and are more likely to be expelled or to drop out before high school graduation (Miller and Jang 1977). Untreated children carry their problems into adulthood where they are likely to repeat the cycle of poor parenting, chemical abuse, or other compulsive behaviors.

Barriers to Identifying COAs

Despite the high-risk status of COAs and the clear need for help, only five percent of the seven million school-aged children of alcoholics are identified and treated (Robinson 1989). Some of the problems in identifying adolescent COAs are due to society's lack of understanding regarding alcohol and other drug education. A teacher's own attitude toward alcohol and other drugs can make a big difference as well.

Many educators have denial systems of their own that prevent them from seeing the effects of chemical dependence among their students. For example, some teachers may be dealing with problems due to their own alcohol or other drug use; others may be COAs themselves (see Chapter 6). Other teachers don't identify COAs because they feel incompetent to deal with the problems or are afraid of causing more trouble. They may be unsure of what to do once a student has been identified. Still others fear parental backlash and lack of administrative support. They don't want to "get involved" and be blamed for overstepping their bounds as teachers.

The biggest barrier to identification, however, is the denial system of adolescent COAs themselves. Very early on, these young people are taught not to divulge the family secret. Moreover, COAs who are family heroes believe that their job is to look good for the outside world, so no one will know how awful things really are. According to Claudia Black (1981), eighty percent of COAs are "looking good kids," which is why they go unnoticed. If six students in your class of thirty are COAs, only one or two of them will be scapegoats or mascots who cause classroom disruption and try to get attention. Those two are likely to be identified as in need of help. The other four COAs will either be family heroes, excelling academically, or lost children who are practically invisible in the class. These are the children who are often missed.

Methods for Identifying COAs in the Classroom

Although there are many barriers to identifying COAs, there are some methods that work. Once teachers and school staff feel comfortable enough to discuss openly the topic of chemical dependence and its effects on others, a nonjudgmental and accepting climate can be created that will remove many of the barriers to identification. To feel comfortable with identifying COAs, educators need to receive inservicing on chemical dependence, to gain administrative backing and support, and to establish or cooperate with a Student Assistance Program (SAP) that offers confidential support services for students at risk. Students will self-disclose more when they see that they have permission to talk honestly without the fear of negative repercussions.

Teens especially need to know that confidentiality will be honored. Nobody wants their "business" discussed by people who don't need to know. If teachers foster direct communication and discourage gossip by their own modeling of appropriate behavior, they can establish a classroom environment that feels safe enough for COAs to identify themselves.

In addition, there are a few standardized procedures that have demonstrated beneficial results in identifying adolescent COAs. One of the most popular of these tests is the Children of Alcoholics Screening Test (CAST) (Jones 1983). It is a thirty-item inventory that measures perceptions and experiences related to a parent's drinking. Because it does not depend on an adult's interpretation or subjective opinion, it is often used to screen at-risk students for inclusion in early intervention programs. The CAST can also be used for research purposes to gather data on the prevalence of this population within a specific school district.

Another objective means for identifying adolescent COAs is one item found in the Cambridge and Somerville Program for Alcoholism Rehabilitation (CASPAR), called the CAF (Children from Alcoholic Family) item (Robinson 1989):

> *Have you ever wished that either one or both your parents would drink less?*
>
> *1. Parents don't drink at all*
>
> *2. Yes*
>
> *3. No*

This one question is a fairly reliable indicator, suggesting that an adolescent's *perception* is more important than how much a parent drinks. That is, if Johnny feels confused, afraid, and embarrassed by

Dad's or Mom's drinking and *wishes that Dad or Mom would stop,* Johnny is a COA, no matter what, where, or how much Dad or Mom drinks.

The denial system will often interfere with a family member's ability to label the chemically dependent person as such. Fortunately, such labeling is not necessary when it comes to identifying a COA. When we focus on the adolescent's *reaction* to a parent's drinking or other drug use, rather than on the use per se, we are validating the adolescent's experience without forcing a label of "alcoholic" or "addict" onto the parent.

Helping Adolescent COAs in the Classroom

There are some very specific ways a teacher can help adolescent COAs in the classroom. Overall, the most important thing to do is to *listen.* COAs are guarding a family secret that is bursting to come out. A nonjudgmental teacher who simply listens and understands is a tremendous help. Besides listening, teachers can also help adolescent COAs by doing any or all of the following:

1. Provide important messages about chemical dependence in the family.
2. Respond appropriately to students who are in survival roles.
3. Offer clear information about alcohol and other drugs and about COAs.
4. Provide classroom activities that help kids deal with feelings.
5. Offer opportunities to build self-esteem.
6. Use effective classroom management techniques.
7. Refer any student who needs help.

Sharing important messages about chemical dependence. When the opportunity presents itself, during a classroom discussion or an individual conversation with a student, you can communicate messages like the following to your students:

- There are twenty-eight million children of alcoholics or addicts, and seven million are under the age of eighteen. If you are a child of an alcoholic or other drug dependent parent, *you are not alone.*

- Alcoholism (chemical dependence) is a **disease.** People with chemical dependence use alcohol or other drugs because they have a sickness, not because they are bad people or hate their kids.
- Remember the 3 **C**s:
  — You didn't **C**ause your parent's alcohol or other drug problem.
  — You cannot **C**ontrol your parent's alcohol or other drug use.
  — You cannot **C**ure your parent's disease.
- You are a person of worth, and you deserve to *get help for yourself.* There are many support groups available for kids like you (COAs). Help starts by learning about this family disease, identifying and expressing your feelings, and making positive choices for yourself.

The above information is incredibly important for all students to hear over and over again, so that peers will repeat what teachers say, and the messages will be consistent. Eventually, the COA teen will hear it enough times from enough different sources that it will sink in. Teachers are very influential and powerful adult role models for adolescents. A teacher may be the only "normal" adult in an adolescent COA's life, and what that teacher says can make a big difference!

Dealing with students who are in survival roles. Adolescent COAs need to learn how to break out of the rigid behavior patterns that serve as "survival roles" during childhood. As a teacher, you can help the adolescent COA by responding in certain ways to each of the roles.

The Family Hero. The family hero who is super-responsible and a perfectionist needs to know that it is okay to make mistakes. You can help this student to accept failure and to value self instead of accomplishments. Encourage social cooperation, and stress the value of seeking help from others. The family hero needs help to let go of being responsible for everyone else and to concentrate on being responsible for self. In other words, the family hero needs to learn how to fail.

The Scapegoat. The scapegoat who is acting out, defiant, and disruptive in class is testing the limits. If you have a scapegoat in your class, you probably feel challenged, provoked, and angry. It's important to stay calm, disengage from the power struggle with the scapegoat child, and resist the temptation to express shock or disgust. When you establish clear expectations and enforce consequences consistently, the scapegoat will develop a sense of security that reduces his or her need to push the limits. Remember that the scapegoat is carrying the pain of the family and feels out of control most of the time. An environment that has predictable and consistent consequences—both positive and negative—helps the scapegoat contain the scary feeling of being out of control.

As a teacher, you need to set limits with all your students, but with scapegoats it is especially important because of their self-destructive behaviors. They cannot be allowed to rule the class the way they rule their dysfunctional family, through tyranny or threat of violence. With scapegoats, you need to act, not talk. Talk is cheap to them. They want to know whether you *mean* what you say or whether you're only bluffing. Never bluff a scapegoat. Say only what you mean. Mean what you say. And be prepared to follow through with whatever consequence(s) you've set.

Remember, too, that scapegoats are natural leaders. Providing opportunities that allow them to lead in pro-social activities reinforces success, which they so desperately need. Scapegoats need help in channeling negative behaviors into constructive ones. You can provide this channeling by enlisting their help in class, by assigning them meaningful responsibilities, and by praising them for whatever they do right, even a small thing such as turning in homework on time.

The Lost Child. The lost child is the most difficult to reach. Of all COAs, the lost child has learned family rule #3 (Don't trust) the best. Because lost children don't trust, they've learned to distance themselves from others, avoid close relationships, and withdraw into their own world. As a teacher, you'll need to help this teen respond to, rather than hide from, others.

Cooperative learning activities are especially good for the lost child. Encourage working in small groups, social interaction with peers, and class participation. Lost children often create fantasy worlds and need to be encouraged to use their imagination, creativity, and hidden talents in more constructive ways. They need you to teach them how to channel their talents. One-on-one contact with you or with other students is very important in getting lost children to open up. They need lots of reassurance, praise, encouragement, and invitations to participate. Although it is very tempting to overlook or forget about the lost child when there are so many other kids clamoring for attention, it's crucial not to give up.

Lost children are in tremendous pain, prone to depression and suicide, alienated and isolated from others, yet desperately wanting to belong. Their trust level is extremely low because they have been acutely disappointed over and over again. It takes a long time for lost children to trust that you are not "just like all the rest" who have rejected them. Adolescents who have adopted the role of lost children are well defended. However, if you are a teacher who perseveres with positive attention and who never publicly criticizes, embarrasses, or humiliates them, you'll eventually be successful.

The Mascot. A teen in the survival role of the family mascot is very often the class clown—cute and endearing, but a real pain. You may often feel frustrated and annoyed with this student and yet find it hard to get really angry, because sometimes the mascot is funny. However, the mascot needs to learn how to take himself or herself seriously. You can help the mascot identify and express feelings that lie beneath the mask of silliness—feelings of fear and anxiety that tend to drive the nervous humor. Mascots need to be held accountable for their behavior, confronted firmly, and then allowed to experience natural and logical consequences for their actions.

Teachers tend to coax, remind, or give "one more chance" to the adorable mascot because they enjoy this student, despite his or her mischievous pranks. Indeed, the mascot tends to be very likeable and is not malicious or hostile like the scapegoat. Nevertheless, it doesn't help mascots to indulge them or to laugh at their humor. It does help, however, to confront them about the way they use humor and to teach them ways to use it more appropriately and constructively. When you take mascots seriously, offer them opportunities to make decisions, and give them attention for their responsible behavior, their need to be the center of attention will subside.

Offering clear information about alcohol and other drugs and about COAs. Even though teenagers may not admit it out loud, they look upon their teachers as those "in the know." In other words, teens generally regard teachers as people who have the correct information. As a teacher, you can make a substantial impact on the lives of COAs in your classroom by offering clear and accurate information on alcohol and other drugs and on the phenomenon of COAs. For example, during Drug Awareness Month, assign readings, articles, books, and films on COAs for all students. This gives valuable information to all students without singling out the COAs. It can also provide a discussion forum to explore local resources for help.

Helping students deal with feelings. All teens have feelings and need help in dealing with them. Adolescents in general need assistance in developing a feeling word vocabulary. You can help teens in this task by doing something as simple as asking them to "say" how they're feeling each day. If you're an English teacher, you can teach words and concepts that express feelings. Writing assignments or collages that acknowledge the importance of feelings without labeling them as right or wrong are helpful for all students, but especially for COAs in your classroom.

Building self-esteem. Activities that build self-esteem are extremely important for COAs, but are also beneficial for all students. Teaching students to talk positively about themselves and others builds self-esteem and creates a warm, open classroom climate. Self-esteem curricula which teach that it's okay to think about self and to say no to others can help the family hero develop healthy boundaries.

Using effective classroom management techniques. You can adopt certain classroom management techniques that will help COAs perform better and maintain control. For example, when dealing with classroom behavior (positive or negative), praise or criticize *the behavior,* not the person, and be as specific as possible. For example, saying, "I notice, John, that your margins are even and your penmanship is very legible. I'm impressed by your effort. That's what I call a neat, good-looking paper!" is more effective than saying, "Nice paper, John."

Likewise, criticism that is specific and aimed at a student's behavior, not at the person, is more constructive. For example, "Joan, in this class, students stay seated. Your behavior is disrupting the class and is not acceptable. Please return to your seat" is likely to be received better than, "Joan, you are so disruptive! Be seated!" Tone of voice is also important. We tend to say things in anger that we don't mean. COAs are used to hearing punitive statements said in anger and to being victims of sarcasm. In fact, they may even provoke you in order to experience the familiar. Nevertheless, it's very important for you to express your anger appropriately, resist the impulse to explode, refuse to react with sarcasm, and thus, model for students neutral and nonviolent ways of communicating angry feelings.

Good classroom management will require you to be consistent and predictable and to establish clear expectations and boundaries with fair consequences. This is especially important for COAs who may not experience this sense of security anywhere else in their lives. If nothing else, you can provide a sanctuary for these teens, a place—maybe the only place—where they feel safe and understood.

Referring students for help. If a COA approaches you for help, there are several things you can do. First, your initial response is critical. Don't act embarrassed, criticize the parents, or side with the student. Rather, maintain a neutral, listening posture and refer to where help can be found. Then, importantly, *do follow through* with a referral if the student asks for help. You may be the only person that student has the courage to approach. Develop and maintain a list of referral resources in your community so that you are prepared should a student approach you for assistance. It's also useful to maintain a small library of booklets, videos, and books for COAs. (See "Resources," pages 55-61, for ideas and information.)

* * * * * * *

Helping COAs will improve their school attendance and academic performance. Addressing the central issue—the student's reaction to the parent's chemical abuse—can reduce symptoms that interfere with student learning, such as fighting, depression, and chemical use. Employing different teaching strategies, classroom management techniques, and referral resources are specific ways a teacher can make a difference. By gaining a greater understanding about COAs and developing programs to address their needs, educators can enhance their school's efforts to accomplish the goals of real educational reform: to educate *all* children and the *whole* child.

6 Professional Enabling

As mentioned in Chapter 2, enabling means "to give power to, to allow." Enabling is the well-meaning but misguided protection of users from the negative consequences of their involvement with chemicals. When people enable, the user avoids reality and continues self-destructive behavior.

Enabling is not an isolated event, but rather occurs in a complex environmental system made up of cognitive, emotional, and behavioral elements. Enabling is always well-intentioned, motivated by the desire to help. However, when we enable we are unaware of how our ideas, feelings, and behaviors affect others. We want to "rescue," take care of, protect, and "help" the ones we love, and we don't realize that our behavior is actually *loving them to death.*

Enabling doesn't cause alcohol or other drug abuse. However, it does unknowingly perpetuate the behavior. It's very difficult to break through denial about enabling, because it feels good to think that we are "helping," and it's safer to suppress feelings rather than confront the chemically dependent loved one with negativity, pain, or doubt. In this society, we've been trained to be loyal partners and friends. Women especially have been socialized to "stand by your man." For many of us, it feels like a betrayal *not* to "cover up" or protect the chemically dependent person. Unfortunately, enabling doesn't help—*never helps*—but only makes things worse.

Enabling is at the core of co-dependence. As mentioned in Chapter 2, co-dependence is a condition that results from the stress of being in an ongoing, committed relationship with a CD. Co-dependent people become so focused on the CD that they neglect their own needs. And co-dependence is a growing concern among professional educators.

"Professional" Enablers

Disproportionate numbers of adult COAs end up in the helping professions (Murck 1988). Not surprisingly, many family heroes become professional caretakers (nurses, doctors, mental health workers, educators) later on in life. Even when helping professionals come from fairly functional families, they can quickly learn that overinvolvement with other people's problems can make them feel useful, needed, appreciated, and distracted from their own issues. Constant exposure to students and/or staff with problems related to alcohol and other drug issues can shift healthy empathy to obsessive worrying. The urge to "rescue" and "fix" is strong, especially when we understand the suffering and pain going on internally.

Helping Versus Rescuing

There are some distinctive differences between truly helping versus rescuing someone. *Rescuing* is an enabling behavior that perpetuates alcohol or other drug use. *Helping* encourages personal responsibility. The helper is able to empathize with the CD's fear and pain without trying to fix it. Helping fosters responsibility for one's own actions, and it views others as capable of making good choices for themselves. Rescuing does for the CD what he or she is capable of doing for self, which, in turn, fosters dependence and causes resentment. When we rescue those who have not asked for our help, we take away their power and reinforce their sense of helplessness. This creates an unhealthy relationship dynamic that could be described as a triangle:

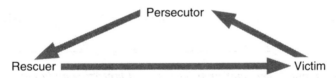

The rescuer jumps in to save the victim from persecution but also controls the victim by intervening. Eventually, the victim resents the rescuer and shifts roles, persecuting the rescuer, who becomes victim. It's a no-win situation. Rescuing, protecting, bailing out people in trouble won't "fix" them but will only make things worse in the long run. Every time we jump in to rescue and soften the blow of reality, we make it that much harder for the CD to face reality. To avoid enabling, we must be willing to take the risk of self-examination and behavioral change. The non-enabler is consistent, sets clear limits and boundaries, and sticks to them even though it might be very painful to watch someone "hit bottom." That's why it's important to be in a supportive milieu, surrounded by others who understand what we're doing.

Self-Test

Here is a brief self-test for professional enabling. The questions below deal with attitudes, feelings, ideas, and behaviors that can contribute to the complicated system of enabling. For each item, mark your response on the continuum. By responding as honestly as you can, you'll discover whether or not—or to what degree—you are involved in "professional" enabling.

I overlook obvious alcohol or other drug problems.

Never		Sometimes		Always
1	2	3	4	5

I avoid confrontation.

Never		Sometimes		Always
1	2	3	4	5

I help to remove consequences by minimizing the seriousness of the event.

Never		Sometimes		Always
1	2	3	4	5

I control pupils' behavior under the guise of protecting and caring.

Never		Sometimes		Always
1	2	3	4	5

I make excuses for, cover up, and defend actions of certain students.

Never		Sometimes		Always
1	2	3	4	5

I feel miserable and frustrated because of an inability to effect change in another's behavior.

Never		Sometimes		Always
1	2	3	4	5

I maintain the "no-talk" rule, never addressing the issue of chemical dependence directly.

Never		Sometimes		Always
1	2	3	4	5

I view alcohol and other drug problems as character flaws and lack of willpower.

Never		Sometimes		Always
1	2	3	4	5

I gossip about students' home situations.

Never		Sometimes		Always
1	2	3	4	5

I view the CD as "one of those people."

Never		Sometimes		Always
1	2	3	4	5

I focus blame somewhere other than on alcohol and other drugs. (The person uses because of a stressful job, or competition in school, or a dysfunctional family, or society's pressures.)

Never		Sometimes		Always
1	2	3	4	5

[Adapted from Anderson, G.L. *When Chemicals Come to School.* Greenfield, Wisc.: Community Recovery Press, 1988.]

Becoming Effective Helpers

Educators need to deal with their own issues related to co-dependence and enabling before they can help others. Co-dependent teachers who are enabling or overinvolved may measure their own self-worth by how many kids they "fix." Or they may identify with a student's problem so much that they feel miserable too. When a teacher "fuses boundaries," he or she is unable to separate from the other person. For example, a teacher gets depressed when the lost child is sad and withdrawn, as if there were no *boundary* delineating where one person ends and the other begins. To be effective helpers, we must set clear boundaries and limits of what we will and will not tolerate—expectations and consequences. And we need to recognize that we can't fix, rescue, or even help everyone. Saying no when it feels like too much, respecting our own limits, and referring to others is critical to preventing burnout. Kathy's story is an example:

> When Kathy was growing up, her father was alcoholic. Kathy was the family hero and the eldest of three children. She never entered counseling or therapy and, in fact, never admitted to anyone that her father was alcoholic. In her early twenties, Kathy married a man who used a variety of drugs, preferring marijuana and beer predominantly. Kathy divorced him in her late twenties and accepted a teaching position in an urban junior high riddled with alcohol and other drug problems. In response, the school district had instituted a comprehensive student assistance program in each secondary school. Kathy was asked to join the core team.
>
> Soon Kathy was giving up her prep time to lead support groups and staying after school to finish core-team paperwork. Although other people were available to lead groups, Kathy didn't think they were as good as she was. Before long, she was using her prep time to see students individually, and leading three groups after and before school. Students would call her at home in the evenings and on weekends.
>
> Late one night, a student called her in a suicidal crisis. Kathy drove into a dangerous part of the city to meet with the student at an all-night restaurant. The student should have been referred to professional help, but Kathy thought she had everything under control and was pleased with herself for "being

there." The student had been drinking. Kathy smelled alcohol on his breath, but she never asked him about it. The student had begged her not to tell anyone about their meeting, and she didn't want to betray his trust. Nevertheless, for the next few weeks, she worried obsessively about him and developed frequent headaches. A month later the student stole his parents' car while drunk and wrecked it joyriding. Kathy became depressed, blaming herself for the accident.

Kathy's co-dependence was interfering with her ability to help. She felt like a martyr but wasn't saying no when she needed to. She was taking on too much, beyond what she was trained to do, and not allowing others to assist her. She was trying to control her student's behavior while ignoring the obvious chemical use. Kathy's boundaries were unclear, allowing students to call her at home instead of referring them to crisis centers or counseling resources. She was in way over her head, and it took a toll on her physically and emotionally.

Blocks to Effective Helping

Enabling factors that most frequently block effective helping include:

- possessing inadequate training in alcohol and other drug concepts and skills

- failing to ask specific and direct questions about alcohol and other drug use

- minimizing or ignoring the seriousness of a person's chemical use

- believing that some alcohol use by students is acceptable and inevitable ("rites of passage")

- attempting to stop a student's alcohol or other drug use alone, without involving others

- failing to refer students who need help to appropriate community agencies and/or for professional help

Avoiding "Professional" Enabling

Educators can avoid professional enabling by:

- confronting inappropriate behavior
- preserving logical consequences for actions
- listening
- showing concern
- being consistent
- setting limits
- defining expectations
- self-care

As a caregiver, probably the most important thing you can do is to take care of yourself. Helping professionals are vulnerable to developing co-dependent symptoms. Addressing your own needs first is the key to leading a healthy and productive life.

When it comes to helping, a wise person once wrote:

> My role as helper is not to do things for the person I am trying to help, but *to be* things; not to try to control and change his actions, but through understanding and awareness, to change my reactions. I will change my negatives to positives; fear to faith; contempt for what he does to respect for the potential within him; hostility to understanding; and manipulation or overprotectiveness to release with love, not trying to make him fit a standard or image, but giving him an opportunity to pursue his own destiny, regardless of what his choice may be.
>
> (Anonymous)

7 Hope

COAs are survivors. They have many positive traits and resiliency skills that help them overcome incredible odds. These children have learned to be leaders, creative problem solvers, resourceful, imaginative, responsible, compassionate, and loyal. In a longitudinal study, David Hawkins et al. 1985, identified risk factors and protective factors that either contribute to or deter later chemical abuse. A family history of chemical abuse is a major risk factor, but not every COA becomes chemically dependent. What makes one child turn to alcohol or other drugs or to other self-destructive behaviors while another in the same family grows up relatively healthy and happy, unscathed by the family's dysfunction?

Resilient children possess social competence, problem-solving skills, autonomy, and a sense of purpose and future. They have developed qualities of responsiveness, flexibility, empathy, communication skills, critical thinking, internal locus of control, and healthy expectations for themselves and others. They learn these characteristics of resiliency in their immediate caregiving environment—if not in the home, then in the community. Hawkins identified *bonding with a significant caring adult* as the most powerful deterrent to chemical abuse. When children can reach outside the dysfunctional family to form a trusting, intimate relationship with an adult who models appropriate behavior, they learn how to "talk, feel, and trust." When children are given the skills and opportunities for success and are then appreciated for their contributions, they form a connectedness with others that builds a positive sense of self. Bonding coupled with clear no-use norms creates the protective armor all kids need to resist drugs.

Teachers have an enormous influence on children. A child has more contact with a teacher than with any other adult except a parent. The relationship a teacher has with a student may be pivotal in forming pro-social behavior and positive self-esteem, offering the protection that makes the difference between the resilient and the destructive child. A caring teacher may be the first person in a COA's life to convey the message "I believe in you. I think you are worthwhile." Caring teachers, without even knowing it, are tossing life jackets and lifelines to hundreds of kids who might otherwise drown in the turbulent seas of the chemically dependent family. Teachers are in a position to dramatically affect students by creating environments characterized by caring, high expectations, and opportunities for participation and recognition. Armed with knowledge, understanding, insight, and access to materials, teachers can offer hope for children of chemically dependent people.

Resources

For Staff

Films and Videos

Children of Alcoholics. 38 minutes. 1982. Features Dr. Robert Ackerman discussing the special treatment needs in working with children of alcoholics and their families. Addiction Research and Consulting Services, 828 Grant St., Indiana, PA 15701.

Children of Alcoholics. 30 minutes. 1981. Features Sharon Wegscheider-Cruse discussing the survival roles in a dysfunctional family. Onsite Training and Consulting, Inc., 2820 W. Main St., Rapid City, SD 57702.

Children of Denial. 28 minutes. VHS. Features Dr. Claudia Black discussing the denial present in COAs and the cardinal family survival rules: Don't talk, don't feel, don't trust. MAC, 5005 E. 39th Ave., Denver, CO 80207.

A Child's View. 36 minutes. 1987. Features Dr. Claudia Black explaining alcohol and drug abuse to children through the use of pictures. MAC, 5005 E. 39th Ave., Denver, CO 80207.

Different Like Me. 30 minutes. 1990. Dramatizes the story of Jason, a teenage child of an alcoholic who lives in two worlds—the pleasant atmosphere of high school and the chaotic world of his home. Johnson Institute, 7205 Ohms Lane, Minneapolis, MN 55439-2159.

A Family Talks about Alcohol. 30 minutes. 1983. A drama about a family with one alcoholic member geared to junior high/high school audience. Perennial Education, Inc., 1560 Sherman Ave., Suite 100, Evanston, IL 60201.

Francesca Baby. 45 minutes. 1981. A drama about two daughters, ages 16 and 10, and the effects their mother's alcoholism has on them. Geared to adolescent or adult audience. Walt Disney Studios, Burbank, CA 91505.

Hope for the Children. 28 minutes. 1984. Portrays problems faced by 5- to 12-year-old COAs and excerpts from therapy groups designed to train adults to intervene. Health Communications, Inc., 3201 SW 15th St., Deerfield Beach, FL 33442-8190.

Lots of Kids Like Us. 28 minutes. 1983. A drama about a 10-year-old boy and his younger sister attempting to cope with their father's alcoholism. Geared to elementary school-age audience emphasizing the messages "It's not your fault," "Stay safe," and "You are not alone." Gerald T. Rogers Productions, Inc., 5225 Old Orchard Rd., Suite 23, Skokie, IL 60077.

Roles. 42 minutes. 1987. Features Dr. Claudia Black discussing the roles in a dysfunctional family. MAC, 5005 E. 39th Ave., Denver, CO 80207.

She Drinks a Little. 31 minutes. 1981. A drama about teenage Cindy who has an alcoholic mother who is destroying their lives. With the help of a classmate with a similar problem, Cindy discovers Alateen and help. Learning Corporation of America, 1350 Avenue of the Americas, New York, NY 10019.

Soft Is the Heart of the Child. 30 minutes. 1980. Portrays the negative effects of alcoholism on the family, including violence and psychological trauma. Geared to adult audience, especially school personnel. Gerald T. Rogers Productions, Inc., 5225 Old Orchard Rd., Suite 23, Skokie, IL 60077.

The Summer We Moved to Elm Street. 30 minutes. 1968. A drama about a 9-year-old daughter of an alcoholic and how she views her family. McGraw-Hill Films, 330 W. 42nd St., New York, NY 10036.

Books

Ackerman, R.J. *Children of Alcoholics: Bibliography and Resource Guide.* 3rd edition. Deerfield Beach, FL: Health Communications, 1987.

——. *Children of Alcoholics: A Guidebook for Educators, Therapists, and Parents.* Holmes Beach, FL: Learning Publications, 1978.

——. *Growing in the Shadow.* Deerfield Beach, FL: Health Communications, 1986.

Anderson, G.L. *When Chemicals Come to School.* Greenfield, Wisc.: Community Recovery Press, 1988.

Beck, A. *Cognitive Therapy and the Emotional Disorders.* New York: International Universities Press, 1976.

Bepko, C. *The Responsibility Trap: A Blueprint for Treating the Alcoholic Family.* New York: Free Press, 1985.

Black, Claudia. *It Will Never Happen to Me.* Denver: MAC Publishing, 1981.

——. *Repeat After Me.* Denver: MAC Publishing, 1985.

Brown, S. *Treating Adult Children of Alcoholics: A Developmental Perspective.* New York: John Wiley & Sons, 1988.

Children of Alcoholics Foundation. *Directory of National Resources for Children of Alcoholics.* New York: COA Foundation, 1986.

Cork, R.M. *The Forgotten Children.* Toronto: Alcohol and Drug Addiction Research Foundation, 1969.

Crowley, J.F. *Alliance for Change: A Plan for Community Action on Adolescent Drug Abuse.* Minneapolis: Community Intervention, Inc., 1984.

Dean, A.E. *Once Upon a Time: Stories from Adult Children.* Center City, MN: Hazelden Foundation, 1987.

Deutsch, C. *Broken Bottles, Broken Dreams: Understanding and Helping the Children of Alcoholics.* New York: Teachers College Press, 1982.

Dulfano, C. Families, *Alcoholism, and Recovery—Ten Stories.* Center City, MN: Hazelden Foundation, 1982.

Gravitz, H. *Children of Alcoholics Handbook: Who They Are, What They Experience, How They Recover.* South Laguna, CA: The National Association for Children of Alcoholics, 1985.

Hammond, M. *Children of Alcoholics in Play Therapy.* Deerfield Beach, FL: Health Communications, 1985.

Hastings, J.M. *An Elephant in the Living Room: A Guide for Working with Children of Alcoholics.* Minneapolis: CompCare Publications, 1983.

Health Communications. *Changing Legacies: Growing Up in an Alcoholic Home.* Deerfield Beach, FL: Health Communications, 1984.

Lawson, G., J.S. Peterson, and A. Lawson. *Alcoholism and the Family: A Guide to Treatment and Prevention.* Rockville, MD: Aspen Systems, 1983.

Lewis, D.C., and C.N. Williams. *Providing Care for Children of Alcoholics.* Deerfield Beach, FL: Health Communications, 1986.

Maxwell, R. *The Booze Battle.* New York: Ballantine Books, 1976.

Middleton-Moz, J., and L. Dwinell. *After the Tears: Multigenerational Grief in Alcoholic Families.* Deerfield Beach, FL: Health Communications, 1986.

Moe, J., and D. Pohlman. *Kids Power: Healing Games for Children of Alcoholics.* Deerfield Beach, FL: Health Communications, Inc., 1989.

Morehouse, E., and C. Scola. *Children of Alcoholics: Meeting the Needs of the Young COA in the School Setting.* South Laguna, CA: The National Association for Children of Alcoholics, 1986.

Reasoner, R. *Building Self-Esteem.* Palo Alto, CA: Consulting Psychologists Press, Inc., 1982.

Robinson, B.E. *Working with Children of Alcoholics.* Lexington, MA: D.C. Health, 1989.

Russell, M., C. Henderson, and S. Blume. *Children of Alcoholics: A Review of the Literature.* New York: Children of Alcoholics Foundation, 1985.

Seixas, J.S., and G. Youcha. *Children of Alcoholism: A Survivor's Manual.* New York: Crown, 1985.

Subby, R. *Lost in the Shuffle: The Co-Dependent Reality.* Deerfield Beach, FL: Health Communications, 1987.

Towers, R.L. *Children of Alcoholics/Addicts.* Washington, D.C.: NEA Professional Library, 1989.

Veenstra, S. *Children of Alcoholic Parents: A Handbook for Counselors and Teachers.* Cleveland: Alcoholism Services of Cleveland, 1987.

Wegscheider-Cruse, S. *Another Chance: Hope and Health for the Alcoholic Family.* Palo Alto, CA: Science & Behavior Books, 1981.

——. *The Family Trap.* Minneapolis: Nurturing Networks, 1979.

——. *A Second Chance.* Palo Alto, CA: Science & Behavior Books, 1980.

——. *Choicemaking.* Pompano Beach, FL: Health Communications, 1985.

Whitfield, C.L. *Healing the Child Within: Discovery and Rediscovery for Adult Children of Dysfunctional Families.* Deerfield Beach, FL: Health Communications, 1987.

Woititz, J.G. *Adult Children of Alcoholics.* Deerfield Beach, FL: Health Communications, 1983.

Articles

Cox, B.B., and E.R. Morehouse (1986). The Role of Pupil Personnel Services Staff with COAs. *It's Elementary: Meeting the Needs of High-Risk Youth in the School Setting,* 414-415.

DiCiccio, L., R. Davis, and A. Orenstein (1984). Identifying the children of alcoholic parents from survey responses. *Journal of Alcohol and Drug Education,* 30, 1-17.

Gover, F.J. (1990, November/December). Children of Alcoholics/Addicts. *Student Assistance Journal,* 3(3), 34-38.

Hawkins, D.J., D.M. Lishner, and R.F. Catalano (1985). Childhood predictors of adolescent substance abuse. *Etiology of Drug Abuse: Implications for Prevention,* NIDA Research Monograph 56, DHHS Publication (ADM) 85-1335, Superintendent of Documents, Washington, D.C.

Kern, J.C., C.A. Hassett, and P.J. Collipp (1981). Children of Alcoholics: Locus of control, mental age, and zinc level. *Journal of Psychiatric Treatment and Evaluation,* 3, 364-372.

Lehr, K.W., and M.M. Schrock (1987, October). A School Program for Children of Alcoholics. *Journal of School Health,* 57(8), 344-345.

Miller, D., and M. Jang (1977). Children of alcoholics: A 20-year longitudinal study. *Social Work Research and Abstracts,* 13, 23-29.

Moos, R.H., and A.G. Billings (1982). Children of alcoholics during the recovery process: Alcoholic and matched control families. *Addictive Behaviors,* 7, 155-163.

Manisses Communications Group (1991, October 9). Study Shows Growing Impact of Alcoholism on Families. *Alcoholism and Drug Abuse Weekly,* 5-6.

Murck, M.E. (1988, May/June). Codependence in the Educational Setting. *Student Assistance Journal.*

Robinson, B.E. (1990, May). The Teacher's Role in Working with Children of Alcoholic Parents. *The Journal of the National Association for the Education of Young Children,* 45(4), 68-73.

Schulsinger, F., J. Knop, D.W. Goodwin, T.W. Teasdale, and U. Mikkelsen (1986). A prospective study of young men at high risk for alcoholism. *Archives of General Psychiatry,* 43, 755-760.

Tarter, R.E., A.M. Hegedus, G. Goldstein, C. Shelly, and A.I. Alterman (1984). Adolescent sons of alcoholics: Neuropsychological and personality characteristics. *Alcoholism: Clinical and Experimental Research,* 8, 216-222.

For Students

Films and Videos

Bitter Wind. 30 minutes. 1973. Department of Audio-Visual Communications, Brigham Young University, Provo, UT 84601.

Children of Denial. 28 minutes. VHS. Features Dr. Claudia Black discussing the denial present in COAs and the cardinal family survival rules: Don't talk, don't feel, don't trust. MAC, 5005 E. 39th Ave., Denver, CO 80207.

Different Like Me. 30 minutes. 1990. Johnson Institute, 7205 Ohms Lane, Minneapolis, MN 55439-2159.

Drinking Parents. 10 minutes. 1982. MTI Teleprograms, Inc., 4825 North Scoot Street, Suite 23, Schiller Park, IL 60176.

Lots of Kids Like Us. 28 minutes. 1983. Coronet Films, 108 Wilmot Road, Deerfield, IL 60015.

Soft Is the Heart of a Child. 28 minutes. 1980. VHS. Gerald T. Rogers Productions, Inc., 5225 Old Orchard Rd., Suite 23, Skokie, IL 60077.

A Story About Feelings. 10 minutes. 1984. Johnson Institute, 7205 Ohms Lane, Minneapolis, MN 55439-2159.

Books

Alibrandi, T. *Young Alcoholics*. Minneapolis: CompCare Publications, 1978.

Balcerzak, L. *Hope for Young People with Alcoholic Parents*. Center City, MN: Hazelden Foundation, 1981

Black, Claudia. *My Dad Loves Me, My Dad Has a Disease*. Newport Beach, CA: ACT, 1979.

Brooks, Cathleen. *The Secret Everyone Knows*. San Diego: Operation Cork, 1981.

Children Are People, Inc. *Children Are People Support Group Manual*. Rev. ed., St. Paul, MN: CAP, 1985.

Dolmetsch, Paul, and Gail Mauricette, eds. *Teens Talk About Alcohol and Alcoholism*. Garden City, NY: Doubleday, 1987.

Duggan, Maureen H. *Mommy Doesn't Live Here Anymore*. Weaverville, NC: Bonnie Brae Publications, 1987.

Hammond, Mary, and Lynnann Chestnut,. *My Mom Doesn't Look Like an Alcoholic*. Deerfield Beach, FL: Health Communications, 1984.

Hastings, Jill M., and Marian H. Typpo. *An Elephant in the Living Room*. Minneapolis: Compcare Publications, 1984.

Hornick-Beer, Edith Lynn. *A Teenager's Guide to Living with an Alcoholic Parent*. Center City, MN: Hazelden Educational Materials, 1984.

Johnson Institute. *A Story About Feelings*. (Coloring book for the film/video *A Story About Feelings)* Minneapolis: Johnson Institute, 1991.

Kenny, Kevin, and Helen Krull. *Sometimes My Mom Drinks Too Much*. Milwaukee: Raintree, 1980.

Leite, E., and P. Espeland. *Different Like Me, A Book for Teens Who Worry About Their Parents' Use of Alcohol/Drugs*. Minneapolis: Johnson Institute, 1987.

Porterfield, Kay Marie. *Coping with an Alcoholic Parent*. New York: Rosen Publishing Group, 1985.

Ryerson, Eric. *Living with an Alcoholic Parent*. New York: Greenwillow Books, 1979.

——. *When Your Parent Drinks Too Much: A Book for Teenagers*. New York: Facts of File, 1985.

Seixas, Judith S. *Alcohol: What It Is, What It Does*. New York: Greenwillow Books, 1979.

——. *Drugs, What They Are, What They Do*. New York: Greenwillow Books, 1987.

——. *Living with a Parent Who Drinks Too Much*. New York: Greenwillow Books, 1979.